A CHILD'S BOOK OF PRAYER

A
CHILD'S BOOK
OF
PRAYER

OLD
FORGE
~

This edition published in 1998 by Old Forge

© Anness Publishing Limited 1997

Old Forge is an imprint of
Anness Publishing Limited
Hermes House
88-89 Blackfriars Road
London SE1 8HA

ISBN 1 84090 027 X

A CIP catalogue record for this book is available from the British Library

Publisher: Joanna Lorenz
Managing Editor: Helen Sudell
Designer: Nigel Partridge
Text research: Steve Dobell
Picture research: Vanessa Fletcher

Printed and bound in China

1 3 5 7 9 10 8 6 4 2

CONTENTS

✝ ✝ ✝

To Do the Will of
Thy Father

✦ ✦ ✦

To do to others as I would
That they should do to me,
Will make me gentle, kind, and good,
As children ought to be.

ANON.

CRADLE HYMN

Hush, my dear, lie still and slumber,
Holy angels guard thy bed!
Heavenly blessings without number
Gently falling on thy head.

✛

Sleep, my babe; thy food and raiment,
House and home, thy friends provide;
All without thy care or payment,
All thy wants are well supplied.

✛

Soft and easy is thy cradle;
Coarse and hard thy Saviour lay,
When his birthplace was a stable,
And his softest bed was hay...

✛

May'st thou live to know and fear him,
Trust and love him all thy days;
Then go dwell for ever near him,
See his face and sing his praise.

ISAAC WATTS

Work a little, sing a little,
  Whistle and be gay;
Read a little, play a little,
  Busy every day;
Talk a little, laugh a little,
  Don't forget to pray;
Be a bit of merry sunshine
  All the blessed way.

ANON.

Goodness, love, grace and gentleness,
Courtesy, friendship and modesty,
Honesty, penance and chastity,
Charity, respect, reverence and truthfulness,
Purity and self-control, wisdom and worship –
All these together are perfect virtue,
    And are the word of the loving Lord.

HINDU PRAYER

AGAINST QUARRELLING AND FIGHTING

Let dogs delight to bark and bite,
  For God hath made them so:
Let bears and lions growl and fight,
  For 'tis their nature, too.

✛

But, children, you should never let
  Such angry passions rise:
Your little hands were never made
  To tear each other's eyes.

✛

Let love through all your actions run,
  And all your words be mild:
Live like the blessed Virgin's Son,
  That sweet and lovely child.

His soul was gentle as a lamb;
  And as his nature grew,
He grew in favour both with man,
  And God his Father, too.

✛

Now, Lord of all, he reigns above,
  And from his heavenly throne
He sees what children dwell in love,
  And marks them for his own.

ISAAC WATTS

Where pity dwells, the peace of God is there;
  To worship rightly is to love each other,
Each smile a hymn, each kindly deed a prayer.

J. G. WHITTIER

'Tis Being, and Doing, and Having that make
  All the pleasures and pains of which mortals partake.
To Be what God pleases, to Do a man's best,
And to Have a good heart, is the way to be blest.

ANON.

He prayeth best, who loveth best
    All things both great and small;
For the dear God who loveth us,
He made and loveth all.

S. T. Coleridge

ERE I LAY ME
DOWN TO SLEEP

✣ ✣ ✣

When my goodnights and prayers are said
And I am warm tucked up in bed,
I know my guardian angel stands
And holds my head between his hands.

ANON.

EVENING HYMN

Now the sun has passed away
With the golden light of day;
Now the shades of silent night
Hide the flowers from our sight,
Now the little stars on high
Twinkle in the mighty sky;–
Father, merciful and mild,
Listen to Thy little child.

✢

Loving Father, put away
All things wrong I've done today;
Make me gentle, true, and good,
Make me love Thee as I should;
Make me feel by day and night
I am ever in Thy sight;–
Jesus was a little child,
Make me, like Him, meek and mild.

Heavenly Father, hear my prayer,
Take Thy child into Thy care;
Let Thy angels, good and bright,
Watch around me through the night,
Keep me now, and, when I die,
Take me to the glorious sky;–
Father, merciful and mild,
Listen to Thy little child.

BISHOP WILLIAM WALSHAM HOW

A CHILD'S EVENING PRAYER

Ere on my bed my limbs I lay,
God grant me grace my prayers to say:
O God! preserve my mother dear
In strength and health for many a year;
And O! preserve my father too,
And may I pay him reverence due;
And may I my best thoughts employ
To be my parents' hope and joy;

And O! preserve my brothers both
From evil doings and from sloth,
And may we always love each other,
Our friends, our father, and our mother:
And still, O Lord, to me impart
An innocent and grateful heart,
That after my great sleep I may
Awake to thy eternal day!

S. T. COLERIDGE

EVENING HYMN

Jesus, tender Shepherd, hear me;
   Bless Thy little lamb tonight:
Through the darkness be Thou near me,
   Watch my sleep till morning light.

✤

All this day Thy hand has led me,
   And I thank Thee for Thy care;
Thou hast clothed me, warmed, and fed me,
   Listen to my evening prayer.

✤

Let my sins be all forgiven,
   Bless the friends I love so well;
Take me, when I die, to heaven,
   Happy there with Thee to dwell.

M. L. DUNCAN

A CHILD'S HYMN

Hear my prayer, O! Heavenly Father,
Ere I lay me down to sleep;
Bid thy Angels, pure and holy,
Round my bed their vigil keep.

✣

My sins are heavy, but thy mercy
Far outweighs them every one;
Down before thy cross I cast them,
Trusting in thy help alone.

✣

Keep me through this night of peril
Underneath its boundless shade;
Take me to thy rest, I pray thee,
When my pilgrimage is made.

None shall measure out thy patience
By the span of human thought;
None shall bound the tender mercies
Which thy Holy Son has bought.

✣

Pardon all my past transgressions,
Give me strength for days to come;
Guide and guard me with thy blessing
Till thy Angels bid me home.

CHARLES DICKENS

Prayer at Bedtime

Matthew, Mark, Luke, and John
Bless the bed that I lie on.
Before I lay me down to sleep,
I pray the Lord my soul to keep.

✢

Four corners to my bed,
Four angels there are spread;
Two at the foot, two at the head:
Four to carry me when I'm dead.

I go by sea, I go by land:
The Lord made me with His right hand.
Should any danger come to me,
Sweet Jesus Christ deliver me.

✢

He's the branch and I'm the flower,
Pray God send me a happy hour;
And should I die before I wake,
I pray the Lord my soul to take.

ANON.

BE THOU WITH ME
THROUGH THE DAY

✣ ✣ ✣

Dear Father
   hear and bless
Thy beasts
   and singing birds
And guard
   with tenderness
Small things
   that have no words.

ANON.

The morning bright
  With rosy light
Has waked me from my sleep;
  Father, I own
  Thy love alone
Thy little one doth keep.

✣

All through the day,
  I humbly pray,
Be Thou my guard and guide;
  My sins forgive,
  And let me live,
Blest Jesus, near Thy side.

✣

Oh, make Thy rest
  Within my breast,
Great Spirit of all grace;
  Make me like Thee,
  Then I shall be
Prepared to see Thy face.

ANON.

O Great Spirit, whose voice I hear in the winds, and whose breath gives life to all the world,

Hear me. I am small and weak, I need your strength and wisdom.

Let me walk in beauty, and make my eyes ever behold the red and purple sunset.

Make my hands respect the things you have made and my ears sharp to hear your voice.

Make me wise so that I may understand the things you have taught my people.

Let me learn the lessons you have hidden in every leaf and rock.

I seek strength, not to be greater than my brother, but to fight my greatest enemy – myself.

Make me always ready to come to you with clean hands and straight eyes.

So when life fades, as the fading sunset, my spirit may come to you without shame.

NATIVE AMERICAN PRAYER

PRAYER

Now, before I run to play,
I must not forget to pray
To Him who kept me through the night,
And woke me with the morning light.

Help me, Lord, to love Thee more
Than I ever loved before;
In my work and in my play,
Be Thou with me through the day.

ANON.

✠   ✠   ✠

Father, hear the prayer we offer:
    Not for ease that prayer shall be,
But for strength that we may ever
    Live our lives courageously.

⁜

Not for ever in green pastures
    Do we ask our way to be;
But the steep and rugged pathway
    May we tread rejoicingly.

⁜

Not for ever by still waters
    Would we idly rest and stay;
But would smite the living fountains
    From the rocks along our way.

⁜

Be our strength in hours of weakness,
    In our wanderings be our guide;
Through endeavour, failure, danger,
    Father, be thou at our side.

                MRS L. M. WILLIS

Saviour, teach me, day by day,
 Love's sweet lesson to obey;
Sweeter lesson cannot be,
Loving him who first loved me.

✛

Teach me, I am not my own,
I am thine and thine alone:
May I serve and copy thee,
Loving him who first loved me.

✛

Teach me thus thy steps to trace,
Strong to follow in thy grace,
Learning how to love from thee,
Loving him who so loved me.

JANE E. LEESON

Look Upon a Little Child

✛ ✛ ✛

Oh, Lord, I am a little child, uplifting
To Thee my hands in prayer.

BIRDIE CANNON

THE LORD'S PRAYER

Our Father, who art in heaven,
Hallowed be thy name.
Thy kingdom come,
Thy will be done,
On earth, as it is in heaven.
Give us this day our daily bread
And forgive us our trespasses,
As we forgive those who trespass
    against us.
And lead us not into temptation,
But deliver us from evil.
For thine is the kingdom,
The power and the glory,
For ever and ever,
Amen.

CHILD BALLAD

Jesus, He loves one and all,
  Jesus, He loves children small,
Their souls are waiting round His feet
On high, before His mercy-seat.

✜

While he wandered here below
Children small to Him did go,
At His feet they knelt and prayed,
On their heads His hands He laid.

✜

Came a Spirit on them then,
Better than of mighty men,
A Spirit faithful, pure and mild,
A Spirit fit for king and child.

✜

Oh! that Spirit give to me,
Jesus Lord, where'er I be!

CHARLES KINGSLEY

GENTLE JESUS, MEEK AND MILD

Gentle Jesus, meek and mild,
Look upon a little child;
Pity my simplicity,
Suffer me to come to thee.

✢

Fain I would to thee be brought,
Dearest God, forbid it not;
Give me, dearest God, a place
In the kingdom of thy grace.

✢

Put thy hands upon my head,
Let me in thine arms be stayed,
Let me lean upon thy breast,
Lull me, lull me, Lord, to rest.

Hold me fast in thine embrace,
Let me see thy smiling face,
Give me, Lord, thy blessing give,
Pray for me, and I shall live.

✢

Loving Jesus, gentle Lamb,
In thy gracious hands I am;
Make me, Saviour, what thou art,
Live thyself within my heart.

✢

I shall then show forth thy praise,
Serve thee all my happy days;
Then the world shall always see
Christ, the holy Child, in me.

CHARLES WESLEY

FOR CHEERFULNESS

O Lord, make me cheerful that I may bring good cheer to others. Let me remember that the world is full of sadness and needs all the brightness I can give it. Give me power to hide my griefs deep in my soul and to bring only happy thoughts to others. Help me to keep cheerfulness as a shining armour always about me, and so shed happiness on all around me. When sorrow comes let me not forget that there is still joy on earth and that in time I shall share in it again. I ask this for Jesus' sake. Amen.

ELISABETH ROBINSON SCOVIL

FOR SYMPATHY

O Lord Jesus Christ, Who wept when Thy friend Lazarus died, give me a heart to feel for the sorrows of others. Make me quick to sympathize with their troubles and ready to do all I can to ease them. When they are happy, let me rejoice with them without envy. Give me such a measure of sympathy that I may be truly sorry when misfortune comes to them. If they are wronged, let me be ready to do what is possible to see that justice is done them. Make my sympathy to be shown in deeds and not in words alone. For Thine own sake. Amen.

ELISABETH ROBINSON SCOVIL

Lord, make me an instrument of thy peace;
  Where there is hatred, let me sow love;
Where there is injury, pardon;
Where there is discord, union;
Where there is doubt, faith;
Where there is despair, hope;
Where there is darkness, light;
Where there is sadness, joy.

St Francis of Assisi

FOR THE UNFORTUNATE

O God, the Father of all men and the Helper of the needy, look with pity upon all unfortunate people in the world. May those of Thy children who have possessions be moved to help those who have not. Touch the hearts of all who have the power to make life easier for those who are in want. Raise up helpers for the poor. Make me unselfish. Help me to see that happiness consists in doing good to others. May I ever find pleasure in helping those who are without friends and in giving without the thought of receiving in return. This I ask for the sake of Him who went about doing good, Jesus Christ, our Lord. Amen.

HERBERT C. ALLEMAN

AGAINST WORRY

O Lord Jesus Christ, Who told Thy disciples not to be anxious, but to trust their Heavenly Father, help me to live without worry. Help me to trust Thee fully and in quietness and confidence to be strong. Keep me from fretting over the past which I cannot change, or worrying about the future which I do not know. Help me to correct my mistakes and to put my hand in Thine and let Thy spirit lead me. May Thy peace which passeth all understanding keep my heart and mind. For Thy name's sake. Amen.

HERBERT C. ALLEMAN

✤　✤　✤

I thank you, Lord, for knowing me
　　better than I know myself,
And for letting me know myself
　　better than others know me.
Make me, I ask you then,
　　better than others know me.
Make me, I ask you then,
　　better than they suppose,
And forgive me for what they do not know.

MUSLIM PRAYER

✞   ✞   ✞

Jesus bids us shine
    With a pure clear light,
Like a little candle
Burning in the night.
In this world of darkness
So let us shine,
You in your small corner,
And I in mine.

SUSAN WARNER

✞   ✞   ✞

ON BEHALF OF A FRIEND

O God, you know I'm often blamed,
When I've been having fun,
And even if I'm sometimes framed –
It's mostly things I've done.

✣

I often mess my bedroom up
And disappoint my Mum,
And when I wind my sisters up
It's pandemonium.

✣

I know you know I'm sorry that
I drive them up the wall –
What worries me is that my cat
Has no regrets at all.

✣

If I've not always told the truth,
Or borrowed Mummy's purse,
Or my behaviour's been uncouth –
My Tibby's even worse.

There's little bad she hasn't done,
And many are her trespasses,
But when she's not committing one
She's really one of the best pussies.

✣

So bear in mind the way you took
My antics and my fibs,
And see if you can overlook
At least a few of Tib's.

STEVE DOBELL

ALL THE EARTH SHALL WORSHIP THEE

✦ ✦ ✦

Let us with a gladsome mind
Praise the Lord for he is kind;
For his mercies aye endure,
Ever faithful, ever sure.

JOHN MILTON

All things bright and beautiful,
　All creatures great and small,
All things wise and wonderful,
　The Lord God made them all.

✣

Each little flower that opens,
　Each little bird that sings,
He made their glowing colours,
　He made their shining wings.

✣

The purple-headed mountain,
　The river running by,
The sunset and the morning
　That brighten up the sky.

The cold wind in the winter,
　The pleasant summer sun,
The ripe fruit in the garden,
　He made them every one.

✣

He gave us eyes to see them,
　And lips that we might tell
How great is God Almighty
　Who has made all things well.

MRS C. F. ALEXANDER

N ow may every living thing,
Young or old,
Weak or strong,
Living near or far,

Known or unknown,
Living or departed or yet unborn,
May every living thing be full of bliss.

THE BUDDHA'S PRAYER

O most merciful redeemer,
friend and brother,
May I know thee more clearly,
Love thee more dearly and
Follow thee more nearly,
Now and for ever.

S<small>T</small> R<small>ICHARD OF</small> C<small>HICHESTER</small>

OUT IN THE FIELDS
WITH GOD

The little cares that fretted me,
    I lost them yesterday,
Among the fields above the sea,
    Among the winds at play,
Among the lowing of the herds,
    The rustling of the trees,
Among the singing of the birds,
    The humming of the bees.

❖

The foolish fears of what might pass
    I cast them all away
Among the clover-scented grass
    Among the new-mown hay,
Among the hushing of the corn
    Where drowsy poppies nod,
Where ill thoughts die and good are born –
    Out in the fields with God.

LOUISE IMOGEN GUINEY

For rosy apples, juicy plums,
    And yellow pears so sweet,
For hips and haws on bush and hedge,
And flowers at our feet,

For ears of corn all ripe and dry,
And coloured leaves on trees,
We thank you, heavenly Father God,
For such good gifts as these.

ANON.

God, who created me
    Nimble and light of limb,
In three elements free,
    To run, to ride, to swim;

Not when the sense is dim,
    But now from the heart of joy,
I would remember him:
    Take the thanks of a boy.

HENRY CHARLES BEECHING

AT MIDNIGHT·OR·AT THE·COCKCROWING OR·IN·THE·MORNING

Make us worthy, Lord,
To serve our fellow-men
Throughout the world who live and die
In poverty or hunger.
Give them, through our hands,
This day their daily bread,
And by our understanding love,
Give peace and joy.

MOTHER THERESA

PICTURE ACKNOWLEDGEMENTS

✠ ✠ ✠

The following pictures are reproduced with kind permission of the Fine Art Photographic Library:
front jacket & p7 *Her First Sermon* by William Holman Hunt; front flap & p42 *Happy Playmates* by William Henry Gore; back flap & p20 *Bedtime* by Dorothy Fitchew; pp1 & 53 *Madonna and Child* by the Master of Castello; p2 *Maternal Affection* by Emile Munier, Private Collection; pp3 & 17 *A Prayer* by Henry Le Jeune; pp8-9 *Maternity* by Louis-Emile Adan; p10 (left) *Learning to Swim* after Arthur John Elsley; p11 *Saying Grace* by Samuel Sidley; p12 *A Game at Baseball* by William Henry Knight; p15 *Amongst the Pets* by John William Bottomley, Thompson's Gallery; p18 *Rockabye Baby* by Jane M Dealey, Beaton Brown Fine Paintings; p21 *A Bed-time Story* by George Goodwin Kilburne, Walker Galleries, Harrogate; p23 *The Guardian Angel on the Mountain*, anonymous, Private Collection; p24 *Fondly Gazing* by George Smith; p27 *Suspense* after Charles Burton Barber, Private Collection; p28 *The Guardian Angel* by M M Haghe; p32 *Idyllic Springtime* by Giuseppe Pellizza da Volpedo; p35 *The Rescue* by Arthur Hughes; p37 *A Portrait of a Young Boy* by Johan Vilhelm Gertner; p38 *The Broken Doll* by Theodore Gerard; p43 *For Such is the Kingdom of Heaven* by Edward George Handel Lucas; pp44-45 *Playmates* by Eugène Verstraete; p46 *Tea Time* by Harry Brooker, Caelt Gallery; p51 *At the Fountain* by H Ward; p55 *The New Kitten* by Paul Wagner, Haynes Fine Art; p57 *The Rescue* by Arthur Hughes; pp58-59 *Sweet Dreams* by Allen Culpeper Sealy, Haynes Fine Art; p60 *Triumphal Return* by Theodore Gerard; p61 *Boys Playing* by John Wells Smith; p62 *The Five Wise Virgins* by Eleanor Fortescue Brickdale; p63 *Jesus Returning to Nazareth* by William Charles Thomas Dobson.

Thanks also to the Visual Arts Library for permission to reproduce the following pictures:
back jacket & p41 *Mother and Child* by E Munier, Private Collection; p13 (left) *The Morning of the Corpus Christi Day* by F G Waldmüller, Vienna, Österreichische Galerie; p30 *Thunderer, a Boy and White Weasel, a Girl* by George Catlin, Private Collection; p47 *Mademoiselle Legrand* by Renoir, Philadelphia Museum of Art; p50 *Playing* by Renoir, Paris, Orangerie; p56 *The Venturesome Robin* by William Collins, Private Collection.

Thanks also to Steve Dobell for permission to reproduce the following verse:
On Behalf of a Friend © Steve Dobell